MW00930948

This Notebook Belongs To

Made in the USA
Monee, IL
13 September 2021

77876697R00068